FOR THE LOVE
DOG BISCUITS

MW00667544

This book is dedicated to Lola, the first gregarious bulldog
who captured our hearts and brought us so much joy and laughter,
and to all the dogs we've loved and lost.

Table of Contents

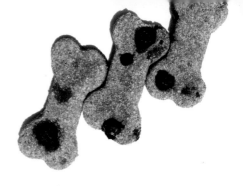

Foreword

A Tale of Dog Biscuits

As a food activist, I've authored two vegan cookbooks for Friends of Animals—*Dining with Friends: The Art of North American Vegan Cuisine*, and *The Best of Vegan Cooking*. **Friends began asking me if I had a third book in me, and after noodling with the idea for a bit, I decided no one had published a beautifully designed, intriguing dog biscuit cookbook.**

So here it is—a dog biscuit recipe cookbook that promises to thrill your dogs (testing the recipes resulted in a number of devoted canine fans) and enchant your dog-loving friends. Within these pages you will find 12 recipes—one for each month—which feature seasonal ingredients and complement the holidays. (National Dog Biscuit Appreciation Day is Feb. 23, and Aug. 26 is National Dog Day if you were wondering!)

As someone who lives a plant-based lifestyle, one of the reasons I was compelled to do this is I felt strongly that the dog treat industry left something to be desired. Since these recipes are made entirely from plant foods—you can rest assured you are feeding your four-legged friends safe, healthy treats suitable for your own palate. And the icing on the dog biscuit—you are extending compassion to all animals.

Dogs were the first domesticated animals, and after they became human companions, their meals became scavenged scraps from the dinner table. By 1895, a biscuit for dogs was developed from a mixture of vegetables, grains, beetroot and remnants of meat, and these were fed to show dogs in the United States as their primary food. By 1907, an American inventor launched the idea of making dog biscuits in the shape of a bone—the only way his dog would eat them—and a year later, they became known as Milk-Bones.

Today, commercial "crunchy" biscuits are scary—full of rendered products from animal tissues and bone (diseased or not), animal by-products, sugar, artificial color (includes Red 40), and chemical preservatives like BHA and BHT, which the World Health Organization has named as suspicious cancer-causing compounds. Also, the state of California has identified BHA as a possible carcinogen.

Most commercial dog biscuits lack moisture and contain chemical preservatives for shelf-life. Other, more costly, naturally preserved pet treats are priced at $6 - $8 per pound and include natural preservatives labeled as mixed tocopherols—derived from palm, soybean, cottonseed, corn or other oils—excluding most vegetable oils. These mixed tocopherols achieve a shelf life for ingredients of approximately one year. (My biscuits will stay fresh at least a week if refrigerated.) However, palm oil production is pushing orangutans to extinction.

In the 1980s, a Friends of Animals' member devoted to her bull terriers, developed a homemade dog, cat and horse cookie line. These treats were packaged in adorable bags, and shoppers at our re-sale shop in Connecticut would look for them as training rewards or desserts on a regular basis. All were full of natural ingredients, but without preservatives they had a limited shelf life since stores weren't refrigerating them.

Would you believe dog treat sales in the United States were $2.6 billion a year in 2013? Unfortunately, today a lot of American dogs are overweight, likely due to too little exercise and copious amounts of high calorie food. It doesn't have to be that way.

Our two rescue dogs Harry and Sampson, the recipe taste testers, compel us to move around and take walks. Of course they get fired up over food and frequent dog treats. But by making a variety of healthy, delectable biscuits we spare our dogs the troubling ingredients found in most commercial treats, and we save money. And now you can too.

It's hard to pick a favorite recipe, but I enjoyed making the Banana and Carob Biscuits. Carob chips are similar in flavor to chocolate; but unlike chocolate, which is poisonous for dogs, carob is non-toxic. There are even gluten-free recipes in the pages ahead, as well as a recipe that can help combat doggie breath. But if you ask Harry and Sampson which recipes really make their tails wag—they would say the Peanut Butter Biscuits and the Peanut Butter Carob-Chip Biscuits.

JANUARY

Harry is a rescued Lab, and possibly one of the sweetest dogs you'll ever meet—with eyes that melt your heart. Not only Harry is obsessed with all things peanut butter, but that's true of most dogs. This biscuit recipe is a real crowd pleaser; even the most finicky will love it.

GLUTEN-FREE

HARRY'S FAVORITE PEANUT BUTTER BISCUITS

MAKES 2 ½ DOZEN 3-INCH COOKIES

2 cups millet flour

1 cup smooth, all natural peanut butter

½ cup rolled oats

½ cup oat flour

½ cup brown rice flour

1 tsp. baking powder

¾ - 1 cup water *(depending on consistency of peanut butter)*

½ tsp. vanilla extract

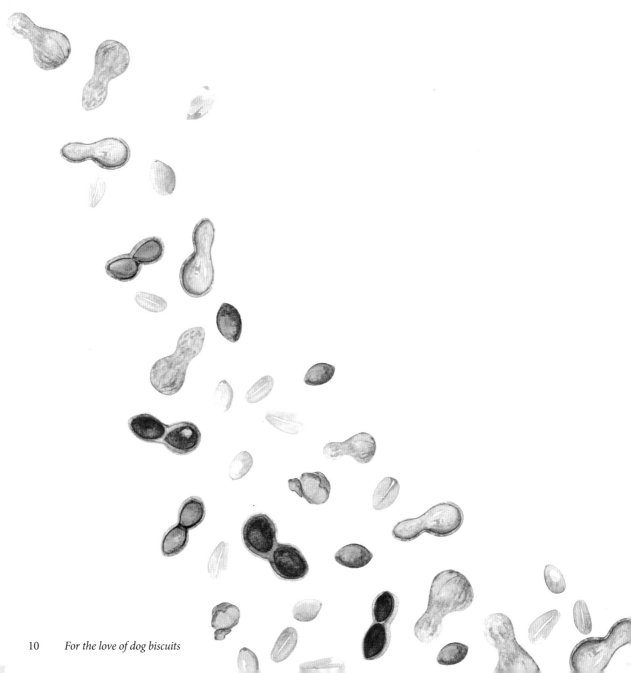

For the love of dog biscuits

INSTRUCTIONS

Preheat oven to 375 degrees. Place ingredients in the bowl of a standard mixer, while adding water a bit at a time.

Use dough hook and mix until the dough comes together in a ball. Add more flour or water if needed. Dough should be firm and not too sticky.

Turn out the dough on flat surface and knead for a couple of minutes until smooth. Divide into two and roll out one portion into a circle, about ¼" – ⅜" thick.

Use a dog bone or other cookie cutter (3 inches or 4 inches), and press out cookies. Lay them 1 inch apart on parchment paper (or silicone mat) lined baking sheet.

Bake in a 375-degree oven for 25 minutes, turning the cookies over halfway through baking. Cool the cookies on a rack before unleashing on happy dogs! Store in airtight container for a couple of days at room temperature or in refrigerator or freezer.

FEBRUARY

Feb. 23 is an important national holiday:
National Dog Biscuit Day.
Harry and Sampson want to remind you, though,
that really every day is national dog biscuit day.

COCONUT-PEANUT BUTTER BISCUITS

MAKES APPROXIMATELY 1 ½ DOZEN 3-INCH COOKIES*

1 cup Bob's Red Mill Gluten Free All Purpose Baking Flour

¼ cup gluten free rolled oats

¼ cup shredded, unsweetened coconut

½ tsp. baking powder

½ cup all natural creamy peanut butter

½ cup coconut milk beverage

1 Tbsp. organic, virgin coconut oil, melted

1 Tbsp. applesauce

* OR APPROXIMATELY 40 2 ¼-INCH
HEARTS, ROLLED AT ¼-INCH THICKNESS

Preheat oven to 350 degrees. Melt coconut oil by heating it over low heat in a saucepan.

Combine dry ingredients in a medium bowl. Add wet ingredients and mix until well combined. Knead into a ball.

Sprinkle dough with a little flour, as needed. On a lightly floured surface, or Silicone Pastry Rolling Mat, roll out dough to ⅜" thickness. Using cookie cutter, cut out cookies and place about 1 inch apart on cookie sheet lined with parchment paper or a silicone mat.

Bake in a 350-degree oven for 20 minutes or until light, golden brown, turning the cookies halfway through baking so they brown evenly on both sides.

Cool the cookies on a rack before serving. Store in airtight container for a day at room temperature or in refrigerator or freezer. Thaw frozen cookies before serving to happy dogs!

MARCH

Parsley is a natural breath freshener,
so if you have a hound in need,
bookmark this recipe.

BREATH-FRESHER
CARROT-PARSLEY BISCUITS

MAKES APPROXIMATELY 1 DOZEN 3-INCH BONE-SHAPED COOKIES

¾ cup minced parsley leaves

¼ cup grated carrots

1 Tbsp. organic, virgin coconut oil, melted

¾ cup whole wheat flour

½ cup corn flour

½ tsp. baking powder

½ cup water

Preheat oven to 350 degrees. **Melt coconut oil by heating it over low heat in a saucepan.**

In a small bowl mix together parsley, carrot and coconut oil.

In a large bowl, whisk together flours and baking powder. Add parsley mixture and blend until flour mixture resembles coarse crumbs. Add water. Mix and knead until dough comes together in a smooth ball.

On a lightly floured surface, or nonstick Silicone Pastry Rolling Mat, roll dough to about ⅜" – ½" thickness. Using a 3-inch bone shaped cookie cutter, cut out biscuits, re-rolling, and scraping as needed. Place on a parchment or silicone mat lined cookie sheet, about 1 inch apart. Bake in a 350-degree oven for 20 - 25 minutes, turning the cookies halfway through baking.

Cool the cookies on a rack and only store in the refrigerator or freezer. If frozen, unthaw before serving!

APRIL

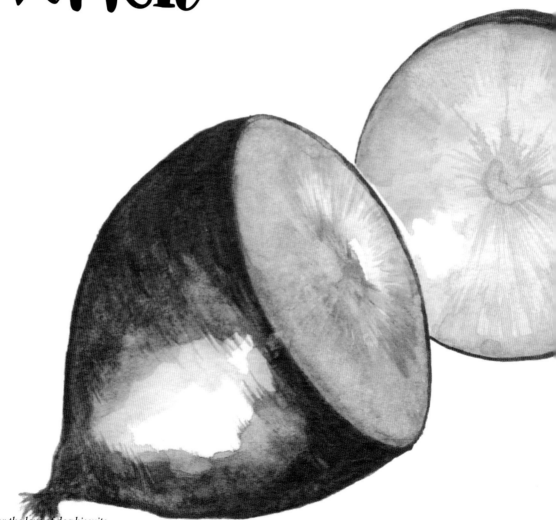

Sweet potatoes are great for humans, and for the same
reasons, they're ideal for dogs—full of vitamin A,
calcium and iron—a real superfood.
And our two dogs, Harry and Sampson,
think they taste super, too.

LOLA'S ALL PAWS UP
SWEET POTATO BISCUITS

2 ½ cups whole wheat flour

½ cup wheat germ

¼ cup Golden Flaxseed Meal

½ cup cooked, mashed sweet potato, or canned Organic Sweet Potato Puree

3 Tbsp. organic, virgin coconut oil, melted

1 cup almond or coconut milk beverage

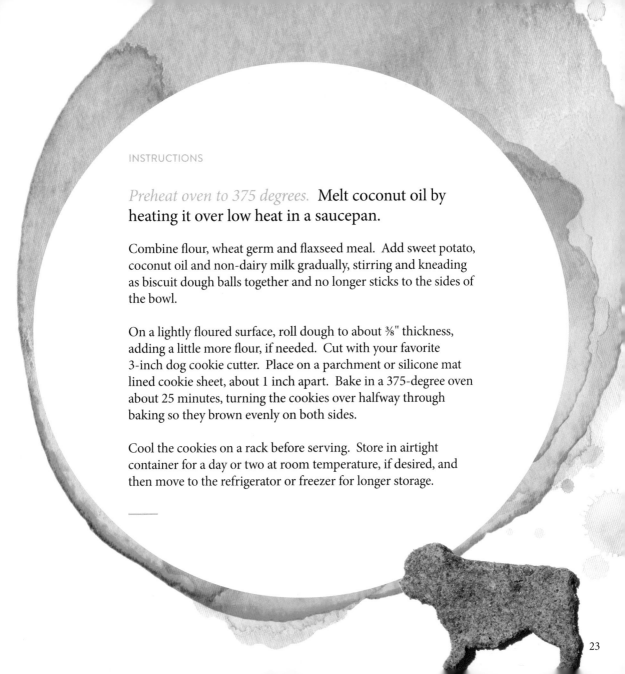

INSTRUCTIONS

Preheat oven to 375 degrees. Melt coconut oil by heating it over low heat in a saucepan.

Combine flour, wheat germ and flaxseed meal. Add sweet potato, coconut oil and non-dairy milk gradually, stirring and kneading as biscuit dough balls together and no longer sticks to the sides of the bowl.

On a lightly floured surface, roll dough to about ⅜" thickness, adding a little more flour, if needed. Cut with your favorite 3-inch dog cookie cutter. Place on a parchment or silicone mat lined cookie sheet, about 1 inch apart. Bake in a 375-degree oven about 25 minutes, turning the cookies over halfway through baking so they brown evenly on both sides.

Cool the cookies on a rack before serving. Store in airtight container for a day or two at room temperature, if desired, and then move to the refrigerator or freezer for longer storage.

———

MAY

Our dogs are big fans of banana in its natural state. Add some carob and other magical ingredients, and it's culinary canine nirvana. Unlike chocolate, carob is a safe, nutritious treat for dogs.

BANANA CAROB BISCUITS

MAKES APPROXIMATELY 2 ½ DOZEN 3-INCH COOKIES

1 cup water

1 large banana, mashed

1 tsp. vanilla extract

½ cup rolled oats

2 ¾ cups whole wheat flour

½ tsp. baking powder

2 Tbsp. carob powder

1 Tbsp. plain coconut milk (or other non-dairy) yogurt

Preheat oven to 350 degrees. Line a cookie sheet with parchment paper or a silicone baking mat.

Combine water, mashed banana, vanilla extract and yogurt in a large bowl. Stir in rolled oats, whole wheat flour, baking powder and carob powder.

Beat dough with an electric mixer on medium speed until ingredients are combined, 1 – 2 minutes.

Turn out the dough on a floured, flat surface and knead for a few minutes until it's no longer sticky. Roll out dough to ¼" thickness and cut into shapes with cookie cutter. Lay them 1 inch apart on prepared cookie sheet.

Bake at 350 degrees until cookies are lightly browned, about 20 minutes for 3-inch cookies, or 15 minutes for mini shapes that are 1 ½-inches.

Remove cookie sheets from oven and allow cookies to cool on pans for 10 minutes before transferring cookies to wire rack to fully cool. Store in airtight container for a day at room temperature, or in refrigerator or freezer for longer storage.

———

OPTION: CAROB ICING FOR BISCUITS

–½ cup roasted carob powder

–½ cup melted coconut oil

Mix carob powder with heated, melted coconut oil. Let cool a few minutes and then dip or apply the carob icing. Place on a cooling rack to harden. To speed hardening, place iced biscuits by single layer in refrigerator.

JUNE

While developing these recipes, our dogs, of course, were the main taste testers; but they were slightly unreliable, because they loved everything. So, naturally, I tried everything, too. So, for the record, these are nice even without sweeteners.

SUMMERTIME BLUEBERRY
PUMPKIN BISCUITS

MAKES APPROXIMATELY 2 DOZEN 3-INCH DOG BONE-SHAPED COOKIES

½ cup applesauce

½ cup canned pumpkin

2 cups whole wheat flour

½ cup Bob's Red Mill Ground Golden Flaxseed Meal

⅓ cup dried blueberries

⅓ cup water

Preheat oven to 350 degrees. **Blend the applesauce and pumpkin together.**

After that's combined, stir in flour and flaxseed meal. Add enough water until dough becomes workable, adding dried blueberries. Dough will be a little stiff. Work the ingredients together with your hands until ingredients are well combined.

Roll out dough to ⅜" thickness and cut with a 3-inch dog bone cookie cutter. Lay them 1 inch apart on parchment paper or silicone mat lined baking sheet.

Bake in 350-degree oven for 40 minutes. Cool the cookies on a rack before feeding to your delighted dogs. Store in airtight container in the refrigerator or freezer.

———

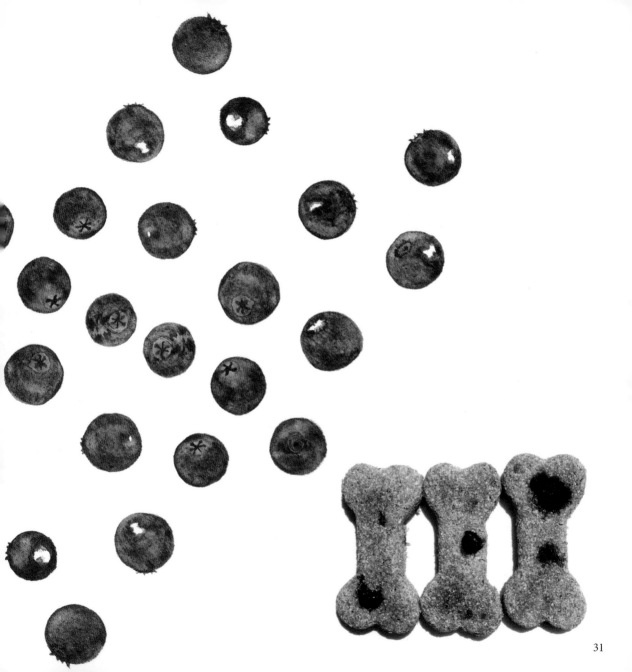

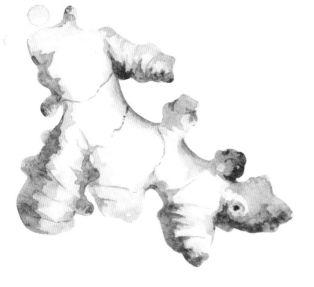

JULY

Ginger is another herb that we look to for curing various ailments. It's also good for dogs. It's said it can help with motion sickness, so try one of these biscuits a half hour to an hour before a car ride.

GINGER NO-SNAP BISCUITS

MAKES APPROXIMATELY 2 DOZEN 3-INCH
COOKIES OR 72 1 ½-INCH BONES

3 ⅓ cups Bob's Red Mill Gluten Free All Purpose Baking Flour

¼ cup unsweetened, shredded coconut

¼ cup Golden Flaxseed Meal

2 tsp. ground ginger

1 ½ tsp. cinnamon

1 tsp. ground cloves

½ tsp. baking powder

¾ cup or more of coconut milk beverage

¼ cup organic, virgin coconut oil, melted

1 tsp. vanilla extract

Preheat oven to 350 degrees. Melt coconut oil by heating it over low heat in a saucepan. Line a cookie sheet with parchment paper or a silicone baking mat.

In a large bowl, combine the flour, shredded coconut, flaxseed meal, ginger, cinnamon, cloves and baking powder.

In a smaller, separate bowl, combine the coconut oil, coconut milk and vanilla. Whisk until smooth. Pour into the dry ingredient mixture and mix until well blended. Knead dough until it comes together in a smooth ball.

Roll out dough on a lightly floured surface, cutting cookies about ¼" thick. Lay cookies 1 inch apart on cookie sheet and bake at 350 degrees for approximately 15 minutes until lightly browned.

Cool the cookies on a rack before serving. Store in airtight container for a day or two and then refrigerate or freeze the remainder.

AUGUST

Harry, and his cousin Bullet, another rescued dog who lives in Brooklyn with my daughter, adore apple slices. They're especially enthusiastic about this biscuit.

BULLET'S APPLE BISCUIT A DAY KEEPS BLUES AWAY

MAKES APPROXIMATELY 2 ½ DOZEN 3-INCH COOKIES

2 cups whole wheat flour

1 cup Light Rye Flour

1 apple, diced into small pieces

⅓ cup organic, virgin coconut oil, melted

¼ cup Golden Flaxseed Meal

½ cup water plus 4 teaspoons more

⅓ cup natural applesauce

Preheat oven to 350 degrees. **Melt** coconut oil by heating it over low heat in a saucepan.

Line a cookie sheet with parchment paper or a silicone baking mat.

Combine flours and flaxseed meal in a large bowl. Add apple, coconut oil, water and applesauce. Mix until well blended. Knead until dough comes together and isn't sticky.

On a lightly floured, flat surface turn out dough and roll out a portion into a round ⅜" thickness. Using a 3-inch cookie cutter, press out cookies, laying them 1 inch apart on cookie sheet.

Bake at 350 degrees 35 – 40 minutes, turning the cookies halfway through baking. Cool the cookies on a rack before serving. Store in airtight container in refrigerator or freezer.

39

SEPTEMBER

Flaxseeds are full of omega-3 fatty acids, which might
make your dog's coat gleam. They're almost guaranteed to
cause uncontrollable tail-wagging.

41

PUMPKIN-FLAXSEED BISCUITS

MAKES APPROXIMATELY 18 3-INCH OR 4-INCH COOKIES

2 ½ cups whole wheat flour

2 Tbsp. Golden Flaxseed Meal

½ cup canned pumpkin

9 Tbsp. water

2 Tbsp. all natural peanut butter

1 tsp. ground cinnamon

Preheat oven to 350 degrees. **Line a cookie sheet with parchment paper or a silicone baking mat.**

Mix the flour, flaxseed meal, pumpkin, water, peanut butter and cinnamon in a bowl. Knead the dough until workable, but the dough should be somewhat dry and stiff. Roll the dough to a ¼" thickness. Use cookie cutters to cut shapes and lay them 1 inch apart on prepared cookie sheets.

Bake at 350 degrees about 25 minutes, until light golden brown. Cool the cookies on a rack before serving. Store in airtight container in the refrigerator or freezer.

———

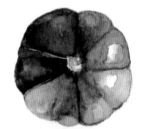

OCTOBER

Sampson, a senior rescue who's part Basset hound and part bulldog, has what some might consider a problem with food. The problem being he's obsessed with it, and spends a large part of his day at the Friends of Animals headquarters attempting to steal co-workers' lunches. He's very fond of carob chips, which are similar in flavor to chocolate; but unlike chocolate, which is poisonous for dogs, carob is non-toxic. And Sampson wants you to know: It's delicious, too.

SAMPSON'S PEANUT BUTTER CAROB-CHIP BISCUITS

MAKES APPROXIMATELY 16 -18 4-INCH COOKIES,
OR 2 DOZEN 3-INCH COOKIES

2 cups whole wheat flour

½ cup rolled oats

2 tsp. baking powder

1 cup water

1 cup all natural creamy peanut butter

¾ cup vegan carob chips

1 tsp. vanilla extract

For the love of dog biscuits

Preheat oven to 375 degrees. Line a cookie sheet with parchment paper or a silicone baking mat.

In a large bowl, combine the flour, oats and baking powder. Stir in the water, peanut butter, carob chips and vanilla until the mixture forms a crumbly dough. Press the dough together to form a ball.

On a lightly floured flat surface, knead the dough for 30 seconds or so until smooth. Roll out the dough into a 10-inch circle, about ⅜" or less in thickness. Using a bone-shaped or other cookie cutter, cut out cookies and lay them 1 inch apart on cookie sheet.

Bake at 375 degrees until light golden, 20 minutes. Transfer to a wire rack and cool. Store in airtight container in the refrigerator or freezer.

NOVEMBER

All the smells of Thanksgiving in a dog biscuit, so naturally
we're featuring this for November. But you can make it any
month of the year.

CINNAMON-CLOVE PUMPKIN BISCUITS

MAKES APPROXIMATELY 15 3-INCH DOG BISCUITS

1 Tbsp. Golden Flaxseed Meal

2 cups Bob's Red Mill Gluten Free All Purpose Baking Flour

1 tsp. baking powder

½ tsp. ground cloves

½ tsp. ground cinnamon

1 cup pumpkin puree (*canned*)

2 Tbsp. all natural creamy peanut butter

Preheat oven to 350 degrees. Line a cookie sheet with parchment paper or a silicone mat.

In a small bowl, combine flaxseed meal with 3 tablespoons water. Stir the mixture and let sit for 5 minutes.

Blend together flour, baking powder, cloves and cinnamon in a large bowl. Add flaxseed mixture, pumpkin and peanut butter. Mix well and knead until dough comes to a ball that's not too sticky.

Turn dough out onto a lightly floured surface and roll out into a 12 x 4-inch rectangle about ½" thick. Cut out cookies using a dog-bone shaped cutter. Place on the prepared baking sheet about one inch apart, baking at 350 degrees about 40 minutes. Turn cookies over halfway through baking.

Cool the cookies on a rack before serving. Store in airtight container for a couple of days at room temperature or in refrigerator or freezer. Thaw frozen cookies before serving.

———

DECEMBER

This biscuit is like a delicious bowl of oatmeal in biscuit form. Cranberries are great for dogs, too, as they can help prevent urinary tract infections (a chronic problem for some). No, you can't use this in lieu of veterinary care, but an extra dose of cranberries can be helpful.

CRANBERRY OATMEAL DELIGHT BISCUITS

MAKES APPROXIMATELY 1 ½ DOZEN 3-INCH COOKIES

1 ½ cups of dried cranberries
(or fresh or frozen cranberries, chopped small)
⅓ cup rolled oats
¾ cup non-dairy milk
½ Tbsp. cinnamon
½ tsp. vanilla extract
¼ cup organic, virgin coconut oil, melted
1 ½ cups whole wheat flour

Preheat oven to 350 degrees. **Melt coconut oil by heating it over low heat in a saucepan.**

Line a cookie sheet with parchment paper or a silicone mat.

Place cranberries in a large bowl. Add all ingredients, mixing after each addition until well combined. Knead dough into a ball and roll onto a lightly floured flat surface, about ¼" thick.

Use a cookie cutter and press out cookies, laying them 1 inch apart on prepared baking sheet.

Bake at 350 degrees 20 – 25 minutes, until light golden brown.

Cool the cookies on a rack before delighting your dogs. Store in the refrigerator or freezer.

———

Frankie

Our Taste Testers

Dexter

Sampson

Lucy

Waldo

Maddy

Zula

Pucci Wu

Ginsberg

Eddie

Penny

Miles

Jake

Edgar

Tyler

Harry

Bullet

Sunny

Monty
& Daisy

Winston

Special thanks to Barbara Sitomer for gluten-free consultation. Appreciation to Brent Arnold for creative help and conception, and Jane Seymour for inspiration, photo-shooting and design. Bob Orabona provided expert dough rolling. I'm grateful to Dustin Rhodes for writing and consulting on all aspects of the book as well as Martha Shaw for offering sage advice. Meghan McIntire provided needed research, and my editor, Nicole Rivard, made the book sing.

Abundant appreciation also to all the dogs and their owners who tested and tasted the dog biscuits. They hail from New York, Boston, Chicago, Portland, Oregon and England. My two dogs sing biscuit praises from Connecticut.